CONTENTS

What is a fossil?

Can you see an animal shape in this stone?

Fossil

These look like the bones and teeth of a dinosaur. It lived a long, long time ago. The bones and the teeth are so old that they have turned into stone!
We call them fossils.

4

Dinosaur Fossils

by Leonie Bennett

Consultant: Dougal Dixon

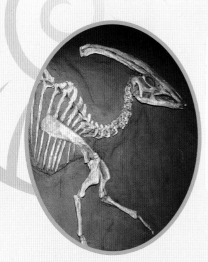

Copyright © **ticktock Entertainment Ltd 2007**
First published in Great Britain in 2007 by **ticktock Media Ltd.,**
Unit 2, Orchard Business Centre, North Farm Road, Tunbridge Wells, Kent TN2 3XF

We would like to thank: Shirley Bickler and Suzanne Baker

ISBN 978 1 84696 611 8 pbk
Printed in China

Picture credits
t=top, b=bottom, c=centre, l-left, r=right, OFC= outside front cover
Corbis: 17, 18, 23t; Ian Jackson: 1, 10, 11, 12, 13, 14, 15, 22b; Simon Mendez: 5;
Natural History Museum: 19, 21t; Shutterstock: 4, 6-7, 16, 20, 22t, 23c, 23b;
Ticktock Media Archive: 1, 8-9, 21b.

This is a picture of the dinosaur when it was alive.

Different kinds of fossils

We can find fossils of footprints.

We can find fossils of plants.

We can find fossils of animals.

7

Why are fossils important?

We can learn a lot from fossils.

We can learn about animals
which are dead now.

Look at this fossil.

Can you see the animal's neck?

Can you see the animal's head?

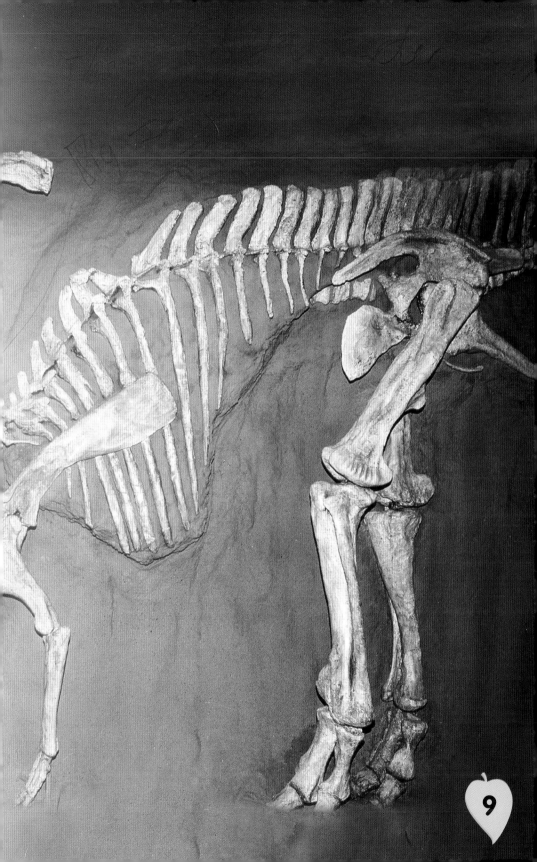

How a dinosaur became a fossil

Look at Hypsilophodon.
It was a small dinosaur
that ate plants.

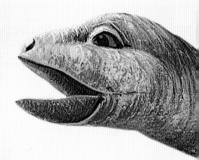

It died millions of years ago.

It fell into a lake.

Hypsilophodon
hip-sil-o-fo-don

Lake

At the bottom of a lake

It slowly fell to the bottom of the water. Other animals ate its skin.

Hypsilophodon

Its bones lay on the bottom of the lake.

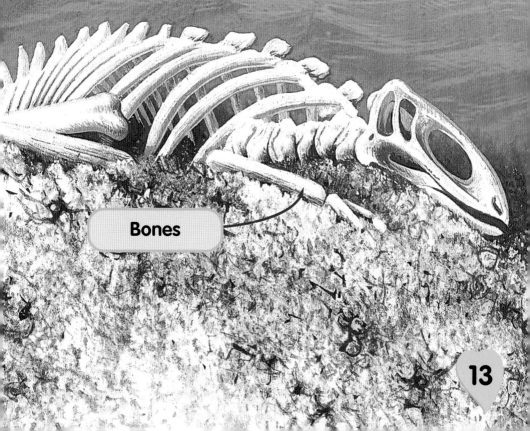

Bones

13

A fossil at last

Mud and sand covered the bones.

Millions of years went by.

The bones turned into stone.

The small dinosaur was now a fossil.
It lay in the rock for a long time.

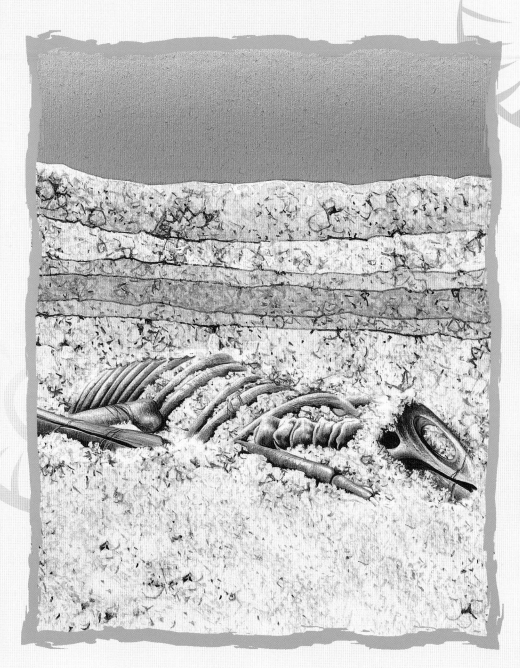

Finding a fossil

After millions of years, the ground moved.

One day, a girl went for a walk on a mountain.

She saw a rock with some fossils in it.

She told some scientists.

The scientists came to the mountain and they dug up the fossils.

It's Hypsilophodon!

The scientists looked at the fossils.
They worked out what the dinosaur
looked like.

They put the fossils of the dinosaur
in a museum.

More fossils

This fossil is T. rex.

Tyrannosaurus rex
tie-ran-o-sor-us rex

T. rex was a fierce hunter.

Ichthyosaur
ik-thee-o-sor

The name of this dinosaur means 'fish-lizard'.

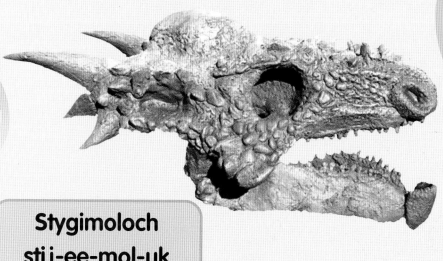

Stygimoloch
stij-ee-mol-uk

This dinosaur is also called a bonehead. This is its skull.

Thinking and talking about dinosaurs

What is a fossil made of?

- Stone • Bone • Leaves

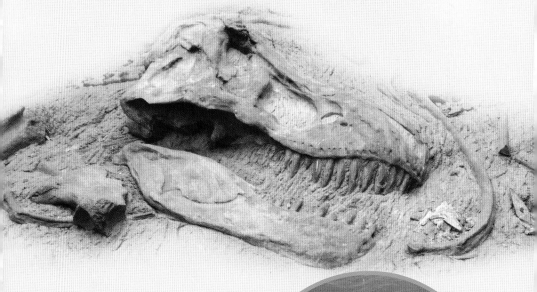

Can you name three different kinds of fossils?

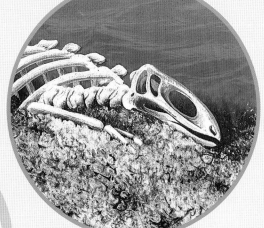

We can learn about animals which are dead by looking at fossils.

Yes or no?

Is this the fossil of an animal or a plant? Why do you think that?

Is this the fossil of a footprint or a fish? Why do you think that?

Activities

What did you think of this book?

 Brilliant **Good** **OK**

Which page did you like best? Why?

• • • • • • • • • • • • • •

Make a sentence with these words:

into • The • turned • stone. • bones

• • • • • • • • • • • • • • •

What kind of fossil would you like to find?
Why?

• • • • • • • • • • • • • •

Who is the author of this book?
Have you read *Dinosaur Babies*
by the same author?